Bradford Washburn
Mountain Climber

by Jeri Cipriano

W9-CXQ-960

Boston, Massachusetts
Chandler, Arizona
Glenview, Illinois
Upper Saddle River, New Jersey

Illustrations
All illustrations: Timothy Jones; 12 Joe LeMonnier

Texts
The Last of His Kind: The Life and Adventures of Bradford Washburn, American's Boldest Mountaineer by David Roberts. Copyright © 2009 David Roberts.

Bradford Washburn: An Extraordinary Life: The Autobiography of a Mountaineering Icon by Bradford Washburn and Lew Freeman. Copyright © 2005 Bradford Washburn and Lew Freeman.

ISBN-13: 978-0-328-67597-5
ISBN-10: 0-328-67597-0

2 3 4 5 6 7 8 9 10 V0FL 15 14 13 12 11

Great Adventures

Is there something you really love to do? Bradford Washburn loved to climb. He first started climbing when he was a young boy.

Washburn grew up to be a great mountain climber. He **explored** the mountains of Alaska and northern Canada. He returned to this area more than 70 times!

Washburn did more than climb. He took expert photographs of mountains. He made maps of the places he explored. He also wrote many books about his adventures. Washburn was a leader among mountain climbers. This is his story.

The Early Years

Bradford Washburn was born in Cambridge, Massachusetts, in 1910. He had a younger brother named Sherry. Washburn and his brother climbed together when they were kids. They started with snow hills in their backyard.

Washburn and his younger brother were early climbers.

Fishing and Writing

For one year, the family lived in New York City. Washburn liked to fish along the rivers there. At age eight, he wrote an essay about it. He wrote about the best way to catch fish.

This was good practice for when he grew up. Washburn would one day write about mountain climbing.

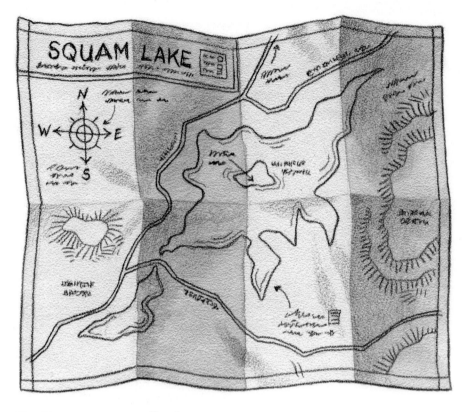

Mapmaking

One day, Washburn's fifth grade teacher showed maps of the world to the class. The maps got Washburn interested in **geography**. He dreamed of seeing far-off places.

At age 14, Washburn drew his first map. It was of a lake in New Hampshire. That is where the family spent summers. Washburn would make many more maps during his lifetime.

The First Mountain

Washburn first climbed a big mountain at age 11. It was Mount Washington in New Hampshire. The mountain rises 6,288 feet above **sea level**. It is the highest mountain in the northeastern United States.

Climbing the mountain was good for Washburn's health. He had bad allergies to certain plants. The allergies seemed to go away in the mountain air.

Washburn climbed Mount Washington with his brother.

A Happy Climber

Washburn's parents told him to do what he loved. When he was 16, his family went to Europe. Washburn climbed three huge mountains there: Monte Rosa, the Matterhorn, and Mont Blanc. Mont Blanc is the highest mountain in Europe.

Washburn wrote a whole book about his climbs in Europe! He told readers to try their best, but to know when to admit defeat. It was good advice.

Washburn's Climbs in Europe

Mountain	Height Above Sea Level
Monte Rosa	15,217 feet
Matterhorn	14,690 feet
Mont Blanc	15,780 feet

Alaskan Explorer

Washburn next wanted to go to Alaska. At age 20, he led an **expedition** there. It can be dangerous to climb mountains. Climbers can die from the extreme cold if they're not careful.

For safety, Washburn always traveled with other climbers on his expeditions.

Washburn's goal on this expedition was to climb Mount Fairweather. This mountain is 15,330 feet high. It sits on the border of Alaska and Canada.

The climb was very difficult for Washburn. He did not make it to the top on his first try. But he learned a lot that helped him in the future.

Success in Alaska

A few years later, Washburn got married. He and his wife, Barbara, went to Alaska. They became the first people to climb to the top of Mount Bertha, a 10,180-foot mountain. The two made this climb on their honeymoon!

The Mount Bertha expedition was Barbara Washburn's very first climb.

Alaska Peaks

Washburn was the first person to climb to the top of several mountains in Alaska. He wrote books about his **achievements**. He told readers that it was important to always be careful.

Washburn wrote, "I was never a daredevil . . . we climbed with a purpose. It was not to show off or set records—there was almost always some science involved."

Pictures from the Air

Washburn also became a mountain photographer. He shot views never seen before. His pictures showed climbers the best routes to the peaks.

Washburn took his photos from an airplane. He would take off one of the doors from the plane to get better shots. The air was bitter cold. Sometimes he took photographs from inside his sleeping bag!

One of Washburn's cameras weighed 53 pounds!

A Hero to Others

Later in life, Washburn worked to help others learn about nature. For 40 years, he was the head of a science museum. He also made maps of amazing places, including the Grand Canyon in Arizona.

At age 89, Washburn organized an expedition to Asia. His team figured out the exact height of Mount Everest, the tallest mountain in the world. They measured it at 29,035 feet!

Mount Everest

Bradford Washburn was a man of many skills. He was a mountain climber, mapmaker, and writer. Through his work, he encouraged many others to explore nature.

Glossary

achievement a successful result brought about through hard work

expedition a long and carefully planned trip

explore travel to places to learn more about them

geography the study of the earth, including such things as rivers, mountains, and oceans

sea level the height of the surface of the sea